SEARCH & RESCUE DOGS

BY PHYLLIS RAYBIN EMERT

EDITED BY DR. HOWARD SCHROEDER
Professor in Reading and Language Arts
Dept. of Elementary Education
Mankato State University

PRODUCED & DESIGNED BY
BAKER STREET PRODUCTIONS

CRESTWOOD HOUSE

636.7
EME
86219

LIBRARY OF CONGRESS CATALOGING IN PUBLICATION DATA
Emert, Phyllis Raybin.
  Search & rescue dogs.

  (Working dogs) 3953
  SUMMARY: Examines the history, training, uses, and breeds of search
and rescue dogs and discusses such organizations as the National Police
Bloodhound Association and the American Rescue Dog Association.
  1. Search dogs--Juvenile literatrure. 2. Rescue dogs--Juvenile literature.
(1. Search dogs. 2. Rescue dogs) I. Schroeder, Howard. II. Baker Street
Productions. III. Title. IV. Title: Search and rescue dogs. V. Series.
SF428.73.E44   1985   636.7'0886   85-18967
ISBN 0-89686-285-2 (lib. bdg.)

International Standard Book Number:	Library of Congress Catalog Card Number:
Library Binding 0-89686-285-2	85-18967

ILLUSTRATION CREDITS

Peter Hornby: Cover, 5, 25, 29, 36
Rebecca Shaffer/National Police Bloodhound Assoc.: 6
Tony Campion/ARDA-WI: 8
Judy Graham/California Rescue Dog Assoc.: 11, 14, 18, 26, 34
National Police Bloodhound Assoc.: 13
Penny Sullivan/ARDA-NJ: 16, 45
Roger Titus: 19
USDA/APHIS Photo: 21, 22, 39, 40
SARDA/ARDA-WA: 33

CRESTWOOD HOUSE

Hwy. 66 South, Box 3427
Mankato, MN 56002-3427

Table of contents

The author wishes to acknowledge the following people and organizations without whose help and cooperation this book would not have been possible:

Rebecca J. Shaffer, Secretary, National Police Bloodhound Association, Dewart, Pennsylvania;

Penny G. Sullivan, President, American Rescue Dog Association, Chester, New York;

Judy Graham, Editor, SAR Dog Alert, National Association for Search and Rescue SAR Dog Committee, Somerset, California;

Bonnie Aikman, Public Affairs Specialist, Animal and Plant Health Inspection Service Information Division, United States Department of Agriculture, Hyattsville, Maryland;

Lt. Colonel Robert Gibson, United States Air Force, Director, Public Affairs, Lackland Air Force Base, Texas;

Jim Webber, USDA Agricultural K-9 Officer, Long Beach, California.

Special thanks to Marilyn Johnson and Twyla Wardell.

1.

Dodger and Watson

"Today, we'll go exploring," announced eight-year-old Todd Adams to his little sister, Sara.

"Can I bring my doll?" asked his five-year-old sister.

"Okay," said Todd. "We'll bring some food in my backpack and something to drink, too."

They were both dressed in T-shirts, jeans, and sneakers. "I'll carry the food," Todd said. "You can carry any things we find in your backpack."

"Don't forget to stay in the fields near the house," said their mom. "Don't go into the woods."

The children walked outside and opened the gate. "Let's pretend we're on another planet," said Sara.

"Yes, in a galaxy far, far away," said Todd as they left on their adventure. It was 8:30 in the morning.

By noon, Mrs. Adams was getting worried. She searched the fields near her house. At four o'clock in the afternoon she called the police. Mrs. Adams was sure the children were lost. "I think they may have gone into the woods," she told the police officers when they came to the house.

Several officers and many neighbors helped in the search. By seven o'clock it was getting dark. The children were still lost. The temperature had been warm during the day. But now there was a chill in the air.

"There's a cold front headed this way, Chief," said one policeman. "The temperature's dropping fast."

"I'm afraid those kids may not last the night," said the Chief. "They're only wearing T-shirts. And it's plenty cold already," he said as he zipped up his heavy jacket.

"They've been gone ten hours now," said one officer. "They may be miles away in those woods."

The Chief made up his mind. "Let's get a dog team in here," he said.

The bloodhound is well-known for its sense of smell, which makes it an excellent search and rescue dog.

Within minutes, a volunteer search and rescue (SAR) unit was called. A dog team was flown to a nearby airport by helicopter. The dog and a handler drove by jeep from the airport to the search site.

When they arrived at the Adams house, it was after ten o'clock and getting colder by the minute. The dog was a female bloodhound named Dodger. Her handler, Ron Marvin, spoke to Mrs. Adams. "Do you have something the kids wore or touched before they left this morning?" he asked.

Mrs. Adams thought for a minute. "I can get Sara's pajamas," she said suddenly. "She wore them last night."

"The nose of a bloodhound is two million times better than a person's," he explained. "Dodger can

This bloodhound and its handler are ready to start a search!

6

follow the scent from the pajamas even if other smells are mixed in."

"Where did you last see the kids?" asked Ron.

Mrs. Adams walked outside and pointed to the back gate. "They went out there into the field," she said.

Ron took the pajamas and let Dodger smell them carefully. The dog sniffed the child's scent. "Now let's see if Dodger can pick up the scent trail and follow it." He turned to the dog.

"Find her, Dodger, find her!"

Immediately, the large red and tan dog began sniffing the ground. Ron opened the gate. Suddenly the dog jumped forward. "She's found the scent!" said the handler. Ron held on to a leash as the excited dog followed the trail.

Dodger led Ron through the field and into the dark woods. She went around trees and rocks. Suddenly Dodger stopped. "She's lost the scent," thought Ron. But then the dog raced off again. The police officers were a short distance behind the dog and handler.

"Look," shouted Ron. "A candy bar wrapper. We're on the right track, Dodger. Find them."

For almost two hours the bloodhound followed the scent trail of the missing children. It was cold and damp in the woods. The scent was strong.

Suddenly Dodger nearly jerked the leash out of Ron's hands. The dog ran straight into the hollow of a large tree. There, huddled and shivering together were Todd and Sara.

Dodger licked the tears from Sara's face. She smiled at the big, friendly bloodhound. "Sara hurt her ankle," said Todd. "We were lost. I didn't know what to do."

"That's okay, son. Everything's going to be all right now," said Ron. The police covered the cold and tired children with blankets. Then they carried the two home to their mother.

"Good girl, Dodger," said Ron as he gave her some dog treats.

It's a happy time when a child is found.

While Dodger was being praised by her handler, another dog was about to start another search and rescue mission. Thousands of miles away, a mother and father were searching for their missing twelve-year-old son. They were on a camping trip at a state park.

"Kenny just went for a short hike before dinner," said his worried mother.

"He was just going to take a look at the creek a few minutes up the hiking trail," said Kenny's dad. "I went up the trail, but I couldn't find him," Kenny's dad told the park rangers.

The rangers searched for several hours. The darkness and rough ground made it difficult. "Too much time has passed already. He might be injured. We'd better contact the search and rescue team. They can start looking at daybreak," the ranger told Kenny's worried parents.

A local SAR (Search and Rescue) team was ready to start searching at dawn. This unit was made up of German shepherd dogs and their handlers. German shepherds are air-scenting dogs. They don't need a ground scent to follow or articles to sniff. (However, many are trained to do both). German shepherds locate the scent of any human being in a certain area.

One of the dogs in the SAR team was a large brown and tan shepherd named Watson. His handler, Rose Burner, took Watson to the creek that Kenny was going to visit. The other dogs and their handlers went downstream along the creek. Rose decided that Kenny may have left the trail to follow the creek upstream. "Find him, Watson," she said to the dog.

The big shepherd ran in front of Rose. Working without a leash, the dog started sniffing around the area. After crossing a large rocky ditch, Watson "alerted" slightly — his ears went up and his body tensed.

Watching her dog, Rose knew Watson was on to something. Each handler gets to know the special way their own dog alerts. Watson got more excited as he moved away from the creek. Watson crawled over logs, around bushes and rocks. Rose followed the dog as best as she could.

Within minutes, Watson found a young boy sitting next to a big tree. He ran back to Rose, who quickly followed. It was Kenny. "I thought I knew where I was," said the tired and confused twelve-year-old. "But I couldn't find the creek. I got mixed up and scared."

Aside from being hungry and cold, Kenny was all right. He patted the big shepherd's head. "Thanks for finding me, Watson," said Kenny as he drank some hot chocolate from Rose's backpack.

"I hiked up the trail to the creek," said Kenny. "Then I saw some beautiful shiny rocks. So I went to check them out. It was starting to get dark and before I knew it, I had walked too far." Kenny was embarrassed. "I was so sure I knew where I was. But I was wrong. At school, they told us to find a tree and stay put. So I spent the night here and waited."

"That was the right thing to do, Kenny," said Rose. "If you had walked all night, it would have taken hours or even days to find you. She turned to the dog. "Good work, Watson."

Rose took the dog's favorite stick from her backpack and threw it off into the distance. "Go get it, boy," she said as the big dog ran off to retrieve it. Then Watson had a game of tug-of-war with Rose when he brought the stick back. "After finding someone, Watson loves to play with his stick," she explained.

"You deserve a special dinner tonight, Watson," said Rose.

"You can say that again," said Kenny as they walked back to camp.

Watson barked in agreement. The boy had been missing more than twelve hours. It had taken the German shepherd less than one hour to find him.

The German shepherd is an air-scenting dog.

2.
Search and rescue dogs in history

In the 1800's, St. Bernards started working as rescue dogs in the Swiss Alps. The most famous of them was named Barry. He saved forty people from certain death in the cold and snow of the mountains. Over the years, the St. Bernard dogs, and the monks who handled them, rescued nearly three thousand people.

In the nineteenth and early twentieth centuries, most sailing ships carried a Newfoundland dog for rescue work at sea. Today, in some parts of France, these dogs are still used as lifeguards on beaches.

A famous rescue dog of World War II was a wire-haired terrier named Beauty. Beauty searched bombed-out buildings in war-torn London. She found many people who were still alive, but trapped under the debris.

Throughout history, bloodhounds have been used for tracking people. Written records from fifteenth-century England describe how they were used to track down criminals. In later years, they were used to hunt for famous outlaws, like Butch Cassidy and the Sundance Kid.

The bloodhound was the first breed of dog to have its trailing evidence admitted into courts of law. From 1900 to 1910, Nick Carter, a famous bloodhound, had over five hundred successful "trails." He helped convict hundreds of criminals. Once, Nick followed a trail which was over one hundred hours old.

This famous bloodhound, Nick Carter, helped catch hundreds of criminals.

The National Police Bloodhound Association was formed in 1963. Its three hundred members are police officers and search-and-rescue people from the United States and Canada. The goal of the Association is to train and promote the mantrailing talents of the purebred bloodhound. The bloodhound is considered a "special tool" in law enforcement.

In the early 1960's, William Syrotuck organized a German shepherd SAR unit in the state of Washington. This was the first unit of its kind using air-scenting dogs. Other units were formed as interest grew. Today, the American Rescue Dog Association (ARDA) is made up of six German shepherd SAR dog units. These units train dogs and handlers using standard methods. ARDA also has a national alerting system for SAR emergencies in states where a dog unit is not available. New units must pass special

Air-scenting dogs, like the German shepherd, can cover a large area.

tests before being eligible to join ARDA or take part in out-of-state searches.

The SAR Dog Committee of the National Association for Search and Rescue (NASAR) represents all search and rescue dog groups around the country. The SAR Dog Committee publishes a newsletter and exchanges ideas and information among the units.

There are about forty independent SAR dog units today in the United States. They range in size from one or two dogs to twenty or more. Many units use air-scenting shepherds only. Other units, especially those used by police, have mantrailing bloodhounds. Some train dogs for both air and ground-scent work. A number of different breeds of dogs are used.

Some search dogs are trained to detect drugs, bombs, and illegal food. Since July, 1984, these "detector" dogs have also been used at airports to sniff out fruits and meats. They check the luggage of incoming foreign travelers. This program was started by the Animal and Plant Health Inspection Service (APHIS) of the United States Department of Agriculture (USDA).

The dogs are trained to alert their handlers to beef, pork, mangoes, citrus and other fruit. The meats can carry viruses into the country which could hurt the U.S. meat industry. The illegal fruit might carry flies which could harm American fruit crops. People caught with illegal food at airports are fined $25.00 to $50.00 (U.S.).

3.

Requirements for SAR dogs

Search and rescue dogs must have an excellent sense of smell. They must be strong enough to get over rough ground. They must be able to work in all kinds of weather. Some dogs have to work ten or twelve hours a day for several days in a row.

The dogs should be easy to train and willing to please their handlers. They should be smart and loyal. They must always be under the handler's control. SAR dogs cannot be distracted by other ani-

A SAR dog must like people.

mals. The dogs should be able to get along well with people and other dogs. They shouldn't be too aggressive (ready to fight). SAR dogs must have the desire to work.

Golden retrievers, Doberman pinschers, and a number of other breeds have all been used as search and rescue dogs. However, most search and rescue dogs today are either German shepherds or bloodhounds.

Requirements for USDA detector dogs

Of course, detector dogs must also have an excellent sense of smell. These dogs must have an even temperament and be well-behaved. They are always around people at busy airports.

They must be friendly and never aggressive. The dogs need to be gentle and calm. They should be small to medium-sized — large dogs may scare the travelers. Detector dogs must always follow the commands of the handler.

Beagles are commonly used for this type of work.

German shepherds

Some people call the German shepherd the "dog of all trades." Throughout their history, these dogs have been bred to be a working partner to people. Shepherds are very smart dogs. They have the ability to be trained for many kinds of special work. Many people feel that they make the best search and rescue dogs.

The strength and size of the German shepherd makes them able to search almost any type of area. They are strong, easy-moving dogs. Shepherds are able to cover large areas without using up too much energy. They can work for many hours without tiring.

The German shepherd is calm, alert, and loyal. They enjoy being with humans and want to please their masters. They have a double coat of hair. The outercoat is thick and straight. It's rough to the touch. The soft inner coat lies close to the body. Their coats are longer and thicker around the neck.

The German shepherd has the strength and size to cover rough ground quickly.

Males are twenty-four to twenty-six inches (60.96 -66.04 cm) tall at the shoulders. They weigh between seventy-five and eighty-five pounds (34.02 - 38.56 kg). Females are twenty-two to twenty-four inches (55.88 - 60.96 cm) tall. They weigh between sixty and seventy pounds (27.22 - 31.75 kg).

German shepherds come in many colors. They may be black, gray, brown, tan, or white. Many are brindled (a mixture of black hairs with lighter ones).

Bloodhounds

Many people believe the bloodhound has the best sense of smell of all dogs. It is bred with a desire to follow a trail of scent. The bloodhound has the special ability to tell the difference between one per-

The bloodhound has the best sense of smell.

son's scent and another's. This ability is called scent discrimination. The bloodhound can follow this special scent through areas which may be mixed with many other scents.

The bloodhound can follow a scent trail which is many hours old. But this is possible only under certain conditions. When the weather is cool and damp, scent is stronger. It settles on the ground and on bushes and grass. In hot, dry weather, scent rises into the air. It gets scattered and harder to detect. It is much easier for a bloodhound to follow a trail in a cool, damp forest than a dry, hot desert.

Bloodhounds don't always work with their noses to the ground. They can take the scent from the air above the ground. Bloodhounds can also follow scent over water. They can even follow the scent of a person on horseback or a bicycle. This is true even if the person's feet have never touched the ground.

Bloodhounds are very good-natured and friendly. Some are even shy. They are among the most gentle of dogs. When they find the object of their search, they usually cover that person with wet "kisses."

The bloodhound makes a good pet. But they need a lot of exercise each day. They have large heads and long floppy ears. There are deep folds of loose skin around the head and neck. Their coat is thin and loose. Bloodhounds are black and tan, red and tan, or tawny (brownish-yellow) in color.

Bloodhounds are large dogs. Males are twenty-five to twenty-seven inches (63.50 - 68.58 cm) tall at the shoulder. Females are twenty-three to twenty-five inches (58.42 - 63.50) tall. They weigh from eighty to 110 pounds (36.29 - 49.90 kg). Males usually weigh more than females.

Beagles

These small hounds originally came from England, and were first used to hunt rabbits. These dogs were brought to North America in the 1860's. They became very popular and are still used for hunting. Beagles hunt alone or in packs. They sometimes compete in organized field trials.

Beagles are good tracking dogs and hunting companions. Yet, they're also at home in an apartment

A beagle inspects baggage at Los Angeles International Airport.

or house as a pet. Beagles are neat and clean dogs. They're gentle with people. Beagles are very calm, even in busy, noisy places. They're patient, friendly, and loving. They have a very good sense of smell. These abilities make them excellent detector dogs.

The beagle has soft, large eyes which are wide apart. Their ears are long. This gives them a gentle, puppy-type of face. Their bodies are solidly built. Beagles are strong for small dogs.

Their hard coats lie close to the body and are of medium length. Beagles have a mixture of white, tan, and black patches of hair. Many are white on their muzzles (faces), legs, feet, chest, and the tip of their tails. Tan or black patches cover the rest of the body.

Beagles are eleven to fifteen inches (27.94 - 38.10 cm) tall at the shoulder. They weigh between twenty and forty pounds (9.07 - 18.14 kg). As is the case with most dogs, the males are usually bigger than the females.

The beagles are trained to inspect baggage carefully.

4.

Human scent

There are sixty trillion cells in the human body. Everyday about fifty million dead cells, like skin cells, drop off. New ones take their place. These dead cells make up every person's special scent. Dogs can detect it, but people can't. Search and rescue dogs are trained to detect a person's special scent.

Scent articles

Clothing that's been close to the body is the best scent article. A sheet or pillowcase from the missing person's bed is good, too. Objects the person handled can also be used. Even cans of soda pop or styrofoam cups give off a scent.

Sometimes a fresh footprint can be used to scent the dog. A piece of sterile (free of bacteria) gauze or cotton is placed on the track for about fifteen minutes. Then the gauze or cotton is given to the dog right away, or it can be sealed in a plastic bag for later use.

The scent article must be protected in criminal cases since it might be needed as evidence in court. It must be proven that the dog followed the scent of the right person, not someone who touched the scent article by mistake. If someone other than the handler has to gather a scent article, it must be lifted with a stick or fork. The article cannot be touched. Then it's put into a clean, unscented paper or plastic bag.

Tracking/trailing dogs

A tracking dog follows the scent where a person walked. A trailing dog smells the person's cells which have fallen to the ground. It may work a distance from the footsteps. "Tracking" is sometimes used by handlers to mean the same as "trailing."

The tracking/trailing dog can point out the direction in which the missing person went. At times, small helicopters will search ahead in that direction. The dog usually starts working at the place where the missing person was last seen. A scent article is given to the dog to smell.

The passing of time can weaken the ground scent. So it's better for the dog to be called in right away. Many trainers believe a tracking/trailing dog should be called in on a search before people start looking for a lost person. This may prevent the need for a mass search effort.

Bloodhound training

The bloodhound is the best known tracking/trailing dog (often called a mantrailer). Other breeds of dogs are taught to follow scent. But it is a natural drive in the mantrailing bloodhound. Bloodhound training focuses on making the dog's scenting instinct even better. They learn to follow one special scent. The training helps the bloodhound concentrate on that scent only. The dog learns to ignore distractions.

Bloodhounds work on a leash which is always held by the handler. The leash is attached to a special chest harness that the dog wears while working. A leash attached to a neck collar might choke the dog as it eagerly follows a scent trail.

Bloodhounds wear a special chest harness when working, instead of a collar.

25

It takes up to one year to train a bloodhound. But each dog is different. Some handlers begin training puppies at eight to ten weeks of age. Others wait until the dog is older.

Bloodhound puppies begin scent training by following short scent trails. Another person may act as the "missing victim." Some handlers have the person show the puppy a piece of meat or other food treat. Then the "victim" goes off to hide a short distance away. The handler gives the pup a scent article from that person to smell. The command "find" is given. The dog should then pick up the

Law enforcement officials use bloodhounds to help search for missing persons or escaped criminals.

scent trail and follow it to the "victim." If it does, the dog gets the food reward and is praised.

As training goes on, the "victim" moves farther away. Some handlers use only praise as a reward. Others use food treats and praise together. For many dogs, the pleasure of following the trail is the reward. After a time, several people hide a distance away from the dog. After sniffing the scent article, the dog must follow the trail to the right person. Sometimes, another person may try to tempt the dog away.

After awhile, the "missing" person may hide up to several miles away. The dog may be given the scent article many hours after the person touched it. Sometimes, the handler mixes in other ground scents to make it harder for the dog. An advanced training exercise could take the bloodhound several hours to finish.

Even after the dog has become a skilled man-trailer, training never stops. A handler will take the dog out on a long trail at least once each week. This keeps the dog's skills at a high level.

Trained bloodhounds concentrate very much on the scent trail. They could hurt themselves by running into a tree or across a street. The handler holds the leash tightly and is always careful to keep the dog clear of danger. Once a bloodhound picks up the scent, they don't want to stop until they find the person. Some bloodhounds tire themselves out to the point of exhaustion.

5.

Air-scenting dogs

The air-scenting search dog detects a person's body cells in the air. The dog's head is held high. It sniffs the air for the scent. The missing person keeps giving off their own special scent into the air. The dog tries to detect the scent from that person.

A heavy rain or very hot weather with no wind, may make it harder for the air-scenting dog. The scent may wash away or scatter.

Air-scenting dogs can cover a large area quickly. Usually several dogs and handlers are assigned to different areas by the leader of the search team. They search areas where they think the person may be, not the place the person was last seen. Scent articles are not necessary.

Air-scenting dogs are also used in floods, earthquakes, or avalanches. The dog can detect airborne scents of people rising up from the snow or under the rubble. The dog detects any human scent in the area, not just the scent of one special person. (Some of the dogs are also trained in tracking/trailing). The German shepherd is the most common air-scenting search dog.

A German shepherd can get a person's scent from the air.

Training programs

All ARDA units go through the same training and testing methods. It takes about one to one-and-a-half years to train dogs and handlers for search and rescue work. Most ARDA search teams have more than one thousand hours of in-field training.

The independent SAR units under the NASAR SAR Dog Committee have similar training methods. Each unit may differ in certain ways from one to another. Some may stress one type of training. Others may have different testing methods.

Puppy testing

Both males and females are used in search and rescue work. Puppies are usually chosen for SAR training at seven to eight weeks of age. An even temperament and a strong body are important.

Penny Sullivan, President of ARDA, picks puppies that like to retrieve. She won't choose either shy or aggressive dogs. Both ARDA and many other dog units use the same puppy tests that seeing eye groups use to select guide dogs. Judy Graham of the SAR Dog Committee uses tests from Guide Dogs for the Blind in San Rafael, California.

Graham starts her testing by taking a pup to a new place. She tries to get the dog to heel beside her on a leash. Next, she tries to get the pup to run to her after an excited "come" command. Then she rolls a small rubber ball and says "fetch." If the pup ignores it, Graham scores it low on curiosity and intelligence. If the dog seems interested but doesn't go for the ball, Graham scores it low on courage. She's looking for the pup who grabs the ball and brings it back to her.

Next, Graham watches as each puppy looks at itself in a mirror. This is another test of curiosity. Graham also sets off an alarm clock near the dog. "I won't pick a pup who runs from a big noise," she says.

Then a stranger suddenly stamps down hard about ten inches in front of the dog. "A good puppy makes sure the foot isn't going to stamp any closer, then goes, tail wagging, to meet a new friend," explains Graham. As a final test, she pushes the puppy down and holds it down. She looks for a dog who tries to get up at first, but then accepts being held down.

Basic training

Training starts when the puppy is ten to twelve weeks of age. Many handlers put their puppies in obedience classes. The dog learns to "heel" on a leash — it walks along on the left side of the handler. The dog also learns to "stand," "sit," "down," and "stay" on command. The puppy is exposed to other people and other dogs during the class.

The handler takes the puppy along on trips to shopping centers, gas stations, and school playgrounds. The pup learns to heel around other animals, children, and adults. The dog gets used to new people and new situations. This is done slowly to build up its confidence.

About four or more times each week, the dog starts to play hide and seek games with the handler and other family members. The command "go find" is used after a family member "hides" as the pup watches. When the pup finds the person, it is praised, played with, and petted.

Soon the puppy starts to find people on command. After a time, the dog can go on short "blind" searches. This is where a person goes off and hides without the puppy seeing them leave.

Daily play sessions are also important for the dog. This includes finding hidden toys and bringing them back, or playing tug-of-war.

When the puppy is older, it can work on five-to-ten minute search problems in the field during the day, and sometimes at night. The pup learns to work alone ahead of the handler. The dog follows the handler's commands from a distance.

By the time the dog is six or more months old, training sessions may last up to thirty minutes in fields and in woods. The dog should look forward to new search problems. The handler must make up new and different practice situations. The searches become longer and harder.

The dog should return to the handler after a "find." If the dog doesn't return, the handler calls it back. Then the dog leads the handler to the find (called a refind). Ball-playing, stick-playing, and words of praise are used as search rewards. After a time, night search problems are practiced regularly.

Agility training

Agility training helps get the dog ready for rough ground on a search. The dog may need to go under

A German shepherd goes through part of an agility course.

fences, over logs, across streams, or climb wet,
slippery rocks. Agility training gives the dog confidence. The dog learns how to move slowly and bal-
ance itself on moving or uneven surfaces.

Some SAR units build their own agility courses.
They may be made of barrels, hay bales, balanced
boards, or piles of brush. Others may have chicken
wire, an A-frame to jump over, window jumps,
ladders, and slides. After awhile, the dogs enjoy going
through the agility course and look forward to it.

Disaster training

Many SAR units teach air-scenting dogs to locate
people buried under rubble or debris. This is impor-

Air-scenting dogs are taught to find people buried under debris.

tant after an earthquake, fire, flood, or other accident. Some handlers practice in empty, partly-wrecked buildings, filled with debris. A person hides somewhere under the debris.

First the handler lets the dog search the building by itself. Then they do a slower, more detailed search of each room or area. The handler watches the dog carefully to see if it detects human scent. The dog's ears may stand up. The dog's body may tense or it may bark. Each handler knows how their own dog will react.

Avalanche training is similar to other disaster practice sessions. However, in this case, a person hides under the snow. As training goes on, the person may hide at greater depths. The dog is taught to paw or dig at the snow if it detects a human scent. Hiding under the snow is very dangerous. It should be done only by experienced SAR units.

Testing

ARDA has made up a series of basic and advanced field tests for its member units. They tell whether the dog and handler are ready for searches. Independent SAR units have similar methods.

In the first test a person hidden in an open field must be found by air-scenting. Another test takes place on a trail through thick underbrush. A person hides about one hundred feet off the side of the trail. In the last basic test, a person hides in a large area of light brush.

The first advanced test takes place in a very large area of thick brush. It's designed to take two hours to find the hidden person. The next test is a night search that lasts more than two hours. The person hides in dense or light brush. The final advanced test involves people hidden in three different places. This test usually lasts about six hours.

In all the tests, the judges watch the dog's scenting ability and eagerness to work. They watch to see whether the dog returns to the handler after a find or

These German shepherds wait their turn to be tested.

if it "refinds." The judges check how the dog and handler work together, and how well they cover the search area. In the last advanced test, the judges watch to see if the dog keeps working after it has found more than one person. They also note if the dog loses interest after many hours of searching, or if it's still eager.

6.

Training methods for detector dogs

The beagles used in the USDA detector dog program are trained at Lackland Air Force Base in Texas. When they arrive, the dogs are assigned to one handler. The dog and handler are trained as a team for twelve weeks. Basic obedience is the first part of the training program. The dogs are taught to "heel," "sit down," "stay," and "come."

The beagles are then taught to find fruits and meats by smell. They connect praise or a reward with the things they are supposed to find. This is done by repeating the lesson again and again until the dog gets it right.

Dogs are corrected with a "no" command or sometimes a jerk on the leash. If the dog is wrong, not giving a reward is a correction. When the dog does the right thing, praise and rewards are given instantly. USDA detector dogs get food treats as rewards.

The dog is taught to find fruits and meat by being walked past open, empty boxes, bags, and suitcases. Then an orange is placed into one of the items. The dog and handler walk by again. The handler carefully watches to see if the dog reacts to the orange. When it does, the handler says "sit" and then "stay." The dog quickly receives a food reward and praise.

The orange may be moved to another box. The process is repeated, again and again. Soon the dog understands that if it sits by the box with the orange, it gets a food treat. After the dog responds correctly many times in a row, a new fruit is used.

As the dog learns to sit for each new fruit, the handler starts mixing them up. The handler may first put an orange in a suitcase, then a mango in a box, for example.

After awhile, the dog is taught to alert the handler to fruit inside closed boxes and suitcases. Then the boxes and suitcases are placed on a conveyor belt which is not moving. The exercises are repeated. Finally, the dogs alert to the packages containing fruit on a moving conveyor belt. The belts are similar to those used in airports.

Next, meats are introduced. One at a time, a type of meat is placed in the open boxes or suitcases. When the dog reacts to the meat, the commands "sit" and "stay" are given by the handler. The dog gets a food reward and praise. The exercise is repeated over and over again. Many kinds of meat are used. After awhile the meats are put in closed boxes and suitcases. The luggage is put on non-moving, then moving, conveyor belts.

Some dogs will even paw at a piece of luggage containing fruit or meat. If they do, they are immediately given praise and their food reward.

Beagles are trained to find meats and fruit hidden in luggage.

Beagles on the job

USDA detector dogs work at major airports around the country. The dogs range in age from one-and-a-half to four years. These beagles wear bright green jackets and are always on a leash. The dogs rest about twenty minutes every hour during their work day. They are returned to their kennels each evening and picked up again the next morning for work. The beagles are not fed until after they are done working. So, during the day they look forward to their food rewards.

When a dog "alerts" to a piece of luggage, a green

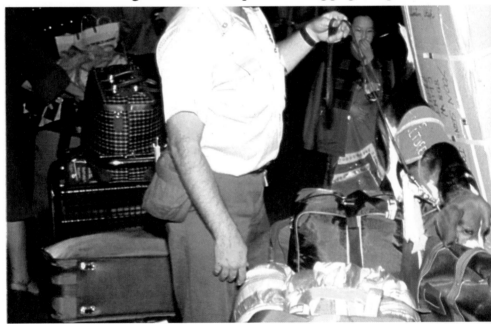

Beagles work at all major airports in the United States.

tag is placed on the bag by the handler. Then the handler marks a green "A" on the traveler's Customs Declaration Card. The Customs officers inspect the luggage. Then an officer from the USDA also checks it. If illegal material is found, it is taken away. Travelers must pay a fine if they were trying to sneak illegal food into the United States. People who tell the customs officers about the food before an inspection do not have to pay a fine.

Each beagle is expected to work for eight to ten years. The dog's last handler can keep it as a pet when it retires from work.

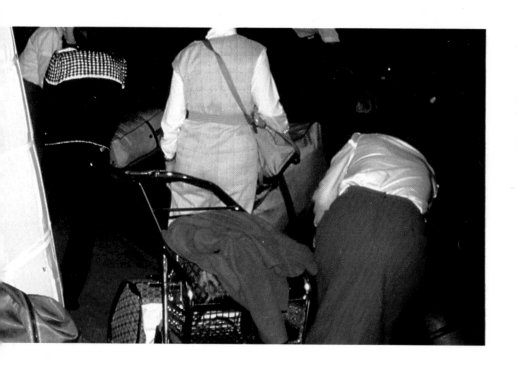

7.

Handlers

Search and rescue dog handlers enjoy working with dogs. They like to be outside in all kinds of weather. Handlers are in good physical shape. They're ready to answer emergencies at all hours of the day and night.

Handlers learn how to survive in the wilderness and are able to use two-way radios. They know first aid and how to read a map and compass. Handlers study search strategy and how a person behaves when lost. They know how to handle special medical problems, such as exhaustion and hypothermia (a lowering of the body temperature). Handlers become experts at mountain rescue. Many know how to ski, snowshoe, and mountain climb.

Mantracking

Mantracking means watching for signs and clues of a missing person. Most handlers learn mantracking. While working with their dogs, they look for signs the person has left, such as broken branches or footprints. Mantrackers must train their eyes to look for clues.

Teamwork

The handler and dog work together as a team, but their methods are different. Ground-scenting dogs, like bloodhounds, work alone with their handlers on a search. Usually, law enforcement, or other officials, follow a short distance behind. Air-scenting dogs and their handlers often work with other SAR teams. Each team is assigned a special area to search. In this way, large areas are covered in a short time.

Each handler is in constant radio contact with a base of operations. The operational leader is in charge of the search. The leader reports to other agencies involved. The leader assigns search areas and decides what plan to follow. Each SAR unit is prepared to be in the field for three to five days. They come equipped with camping gear, food, and supplies for their dogs and themselves.

Who is eligible?

Most SAR teams are called into service by public agencies, not individual people. Counties, cities, police and fire departments, or national parks contact SAR units directly, or they call special alert numbers. Some units work through state agencies. Others work through police departments. There is a national alerting phone number for ARDA units.

Most mantrailing bloodhounds and their handlers are called directly by law enforcement officials. Many police and sheriff's departments have their own bloodhounds.

Transportation and cost

When possible, individual unit members drive to the search scene in trucks, vans, or cars. However, the Air Force Rescue Coordination Center at Scott Air Force Base in Illinois will fly SAR units to search sites.

SAR dog units provide their services free to all agencies which ask for them. They are all volunteers and receive no salary.

Money, supplies, and equipment are often donated to search and rescue dog units by people in the community, businesses, and organizations. But many handlers pay all of their expenses themselves.

SAR dogs and people

SAR dogs use their special sense of smell to help people. One dog and handler can do the work of many people. A single search and rescue dog can do as much as twenty to thirty trained searchers. One detector dog can sniff pieces of luggage that would otherwise take many workers to check.

Dogs have proven themselves to be valuable partners in all types of search and rescue work. They help protect industries and they save people's lives.

SAR dogs have saved many people.

45

Glossary

AGILITY — *The ability to have quick and easy movements.*

ALERTING — *The way in which the dog responds to a missing person's scent, usually moving towards the subject with its ears standing up, its body tensing, and sometimes by barking; some dogs paw at something or sit quietly while alerting, depending on how it was trained; the handler learns to "read" the dog's reaction.*

AIR-SCENTING DOG — *A dog which detects the missing person's scent from the air.*

ARDA — *American Rescue Dog Association.*

AVALANCHE — *Loose snow or rock which suddenly slides down a mountain.*

BRINDLED — *Having a mixture of black and lighter-colored hair.*

BRUSH, UNDERBRUSH — *Small and low shrubs and bushes which grow in forests or woods under the larger trees.*

CITRUS — *Oranges, lemons, limes, or other similar fruit.*

CURIOSITY — *To want to learn about things or know something.*

DEBRIS — *What is left after something breaks down or is destroyed; ruins.*

EXHAUSTION — *Being completely used up and tired.*

GAUZE — *Thin and light, loose material.*

INSTINCT — *An automatic natural behavior in animals; an inborn response or reaction.*

MANGOES — *A juicy, yellow-red tropical fruit.*

MANTRACKER — *A person who watches for signs, clues, and footprints of the missing person.*

MANTRAILER — *A tracking/trailing dog which follows a ground scent of a person; usually refers to the bloodhound.*

NASAR — *National Association for Search and Rescue.*

SCENT ARTICLE — *A piece of clothing or something the missing person has touched; it's given to the dog so it can smell the scent and pick up that person's scent trail.*

SCENT DISCRIMINATION — *A dog's ability to tell the difference between one person's scent and another's.*

SNOWSHOEING — *To use snowshoes while walking over deep snow; a racket-shaped wood frame crisscrossed with leather worn on the feet; prevents sinking in the snow.*

STRATEGY — *Planning, directing, and managing a special action.*

TEMPERAMENT — *The emotional characteristics that are special to each dog; its personality or frame of mind.*

VIRUSES — *Organisms which cause diseases like smallpox.*

WORKING DOGS

READ ABOUT THE MANY KINDS OF DOGS THAT WORK FOR A LIVING:

HEARING-EAR DOGS   **GUIDE DOGS**   **WATCH/GUARD DOGS**

LAW ENFORCEMENT DOGS   **SEARCH & RESCUE DOGS**

STUNT DOGS   **SLED DOGS**   **MILITARY DOGS**

CRESTWOOD HOUSE